Are you ready to have four pockets full?

FULFILLING

Strategies on how to remain full
- *Mentally*
- *Emotionally*
- *Spiritually*
- *Physically*

BY MYKA GRAHAM

To order additional copies of this book, contact:
Xlibris
844-714-8691
www.Xlibris.com
Orders@Xlibris.com

ISBN: Softcover   978-1-6641-6931-9
        EBook   978-1-6641-6930-2

Print information available on the last page

Rev. date: 04/19/2021

FULFILLING

TABLE OF CONTENTS

PREFACE

I learned to cope with the troubles
in my life by reading books
while undergoing anxiety &
depression ...writing is what brought
me joy & fulfilled peace in my heart,
helping those in need. Even if it's a
small impact. I would like to bring
awareness to mental & financial
literacy and balancing emotion within
yourself and interacting with others.

Sharing useful tips on how
to maneuver through this
beautiful chaos we label life.

EMOTIONS

Balancing emotions within yourself can feel like a battlefield, completely at war with yourself. You may struggle expressing your actual feelings, afraid of judgement or the possibility that you are fighting what you know against what you feel. I'm here to inform you that you are not alone! Emotions can be a rocky situation. Did you know there are actually twenty-seven human emotions? The emotions we are familiar with are happiness, sadness, fear, anger, surprise and disgust. Now here is the big question.. How can I strive to manage all my emotions? The truth is we are all CEO's of our life and we must hire and fire accordingly. Often our emotions get all the blame in the endgame. Placing the blame on anger, sadness and fear .. But who is in charge of these emotions we so helplessly place blame upon? …. We all know the answer, less blame more accountability.

ETHEREAL- EXTREMELY DELICATE AND LIGHT IN A WAY THAT SEEMS TO PERFECT FOR THIS WORLD

BALANCE:

Balance is very vital, overwhelming yourself can lead to destruction. Happy zones are your balance. Try to adopt hobbies that make you feel at ease and are fulfilling to your heart. How can an individual balance happiness and anger? Anger is within us all and you must subside anger. Its a given emotion which can be controlled or uncontrolled at any moment. The same applies to happiness. Happiness is within.

FIGHTING THE BATTLE SELF VS SELF

How do I overcome this battle?

You can fight the good fight and defeat all odds against you. Be courageous and have confidence that you are capable to do whatever it takes.

RECHARGE

No matter how busy you are, take half – hour each day just for yourself. Go for walk, plan healthy meals or simply relax.

Reconnect and recharge; You are not being selfish. You need the time to focus on your on your own well-being. After all, if you are not healthy, how can you be there for anyone else.

FULFILLING

I stopped looking at things and stopped saying, "I wish that was me." I started saying, "Okay, I can do that too." You have to completely stop comparing and start being inspired, motivated and self-driven. You can literally do anything you put your mind to always remember, you are your only limit. The only thing that can stop you, is you.

MENTAL HEALTH

Mental health is a serious matter and should not be taken lightly. I feel that mental health is often overlooked. I feel that I have been given a divine purpose to shed light on this matter & hoe to deal with triggers on a daily basis.

EMOTIONAL DETOX

Whether you are moving through a traumatic experience, looking to release the past or want to create more positive experiences in your life; Emotional detoxes will help. You may have trouble saying the word "No" yet you are going to have to learn how to decline engagements in order to re-engage with yourself:

1. Be more selective
2. Do you find yourself trying to fix everyone else problems?
3. It is important to fix yourself first.

If you are an over-thinker. Try not to dwell on life's problems are you are in need of an emotions detox.

TRANSFORMATION IN THINKING

DAY 2

TRANSFORM

Training your brain to think in new healthier ways is a process yet know you'll get there. I've been low. I've been hopeless and helpless. I wasn't able to pinpoint at that time which thoughts were keeping me down. I had many negative automatic thoughts that were going unnoticed. Telling myself, "I deserve this" I deserve being disliked and or being unhappy. These underpinned all my interactions with others. I was in a lost place but I found my way out. How? I was introduced to new ways of thinking that took many years to learn and adopt. Although I am better than I was. I'll always be learning. If you're ever felt this way. You are not wrong or strange. Nobody deserves that type of torment, fear and despair that I've gone through. This applies to absolutely anyone who feels the same way. I've been there. Please know you don't deserve any invisible pain and you never did. The human brain is amazing. You can train your mind and be kind. To be empathetic towards yourself and ultimately change behaviors.

EMOTIONAL APPEAL

Letting go and healing means that you trust that the situation is playing out the way it should. You trust your heart to go through it's grieving process whether that may be to you. You allowed your emotions to close for a season and reopen as in time your trueness will bloom again in the spring if you allow it! If it was meant to go any other way, it would have but it happened the way it did and the way it should have and in a way it needed to in order for you to learn the lesson and it happened in order for you to experience your evolution.

FEARLESS, LOVE MORE.

INTROSPECTION

Introspection is looking inward at yourself, your choices actions, beliefs, behaviors, reactions and results. As you learn more about yourself. You gain access to your deepest layers further and further you dig you learn new things about yourself. You dig some more and you discover deep things within that have been hidden for too long. Dwindling down ever slowly out of fear of being too much. Fear of not being accepted or loved fear of the unknown.

The more self-aware you become, the more you see yourself in others. The more understanding you become, the more you lead with love, the more you attract love back.

SELF LOVE

TRIGGERED

Unresolved issues and feelings don't just go away. History always repeats itself until they get it right. Perhaps feelings of jealousy, shame, confusion, guilt, rejection, grief or fear - and I feel you there. We all experience those feelings. The rise and the fall. Don't resist it. Learn to love and honor the complete cycle of your process of transformation. Negative emotions are uncomfortable to deal with. But avoiding those feelings is just a temporary solution to a much deeper problem. You are unconsciously burying passwords deeper inside of you. And ultimately hurting yourself more deeply than you know.

Face what you must face and allow those things unfold organically. You will gradually feel lighter brighter until the pain fades away. There will be no more trying to suppress thoughts and memories from the past. You will wake up one day and be at peace. Please with where you've been. What you've been through and where you're headed.

SELF — WORTH

Self-confidence and self worth cannot be overstated. It must be taught, practiced and reinforced. Sadly we are living in an era where we are relying on social media to gain our self-worth and strive to attain society's unattainable ideal image which has many people lonelier because we are spending out time filtering our photos and real lives, instead of embracing out true selves flaws and all. The truth is you don't need validation from anyone to know that you are worthy.

Exterior beauty is only temporary, the conditions of your hearts, what our character reflects, and the compassion we have towards others matters most.

CONFIDENCE

TIME

Be aware of your time and
your energy it is VALUABLE.

Know in your heart, mind and soul you
are WORTHY of everything you desire.

Don't let time discourage YOU,
you can create greatness

YOU are in charge

Although you may fell like time is fading away or
believe you are running out of time. Here to ensure
YOU, you have potential and go after everything with
love.

WHICH CUP ARE YOU FILLING UP?

ARE YOU FOR YOURSELF OR AGAINST YOURSELF?

LOVE ON YOU

Fill the cup that builds you, inspires you to do better. Makes you more happier, gives you the incentives to be a helping hand to others. The cup that strives you to get up early and drink tea or coffee or perhaps a smoothie and go for a morning walk or a morning run just to produce better version of yourself. Showing more gratitude. Showing more compassion. Showing more LOVE.

Whereas the sup that tears you down and brings out a version of yourself that you would rather hide. The once who can say hateful words and be negative towards yourself and others.

Choose wisely both a reflection of YOU.

Reflection

WHICH CUP ARE YOU FILLING UP?

ARE YOU FOR YOURSELF OR AGAINST YOURSELF?

LOVE ON YOU

Aftermath

- Which cup brings the best version of yourself?

- Are you more motivated happy or angry?

- Which cup has the best impact on others around YOU?

Reflection

WHICH CUP ARE YOU FILLING UP?

ARE YOU FOR YOURSELF OR AGAINST YOURSELF?

LOVE ON YOU

If you can see it in your mind
you can hold it in your hand.

Tap into your GREATNESS

Believe in YOURSELF

Push yourself you are all you need.

You are champion.

Reflection

WHICH CUP ARE YOU FILLING UP?

ARE YOU FOR YOURSELF OR AGAINST YOURSELF?

LOVE ON YOU

Which cup fills you up
closer to your goals?

Which cup enlightens your gift?

Your gift will make room for you,
now that is your gift? It's the thing
you do the ABSOLUTE BEST with
the least amount of effort, Quit
running away from the GIFT.

Reflection

WHICH CUP ARE YOU FILLING UP?

ARE YOU YOURSELF OR AGAINST YOURSELF

LOVE IN YOU

What is the color of your heart today?

Pick up more gratitude and stop and look around the word and be grateful you are alive to experience this life.

You have to change the words you use. When you say "I will try or I can't", you are setting doubt inside your mind. But if you say "I can or I will or I am going to began this project then you are planting positivity inside you"

Reflection

Working Within

Good morning how is it inside?
Are you blue inside? Do you
feel rage? Are you happy?

• Go to the library if needed
• Get therapy if needed
• Talk to therapist about Mental Health
• Work on your physical
• Work on your mental
• Happiness comes from within
• Be confident
• Fail big welcome failure
embrace it if you must.

Reflection

Working Within

Don't beat yourself up over mistakes.
You are human. You will
make mistakes.
Some more apparent of others.
Some were done out of
envy, pride, lust, guilt.
Some are just tiny mistakes and
some big as the Effiel tower.
Perfect is not real there's no such thing.

Reflection

Working Within

What are you struggling with?

BE HONEST

Do you struggle with being slow to anger? Do you have trouble forgiving? Do you struggle with temptation? DO you face a battle of being kind to others. Is it stressful for you to love yourself and appreciate yourself?

LOVE YOUR PLANS

Reflection

When your glory falls let it drive out every fear let it drive out every insecurity

FAITH OVE FEAR

Reflection

Shake the dust of my past off of my feet. Help me to remove the memories of failures and short — comings out of my mind.

UPROOT IT REBUKE IT

Pray for Health & Happiness

MORE LOVE MORE PEACE

Have confidence that you deliver
something no one else can.

SUPPORT YOUR GROWTH

Reflection

Qualifying Our Squares

DO YOU KNOW WHO
YOUR SELECT

Those individuals who
xxx you, support you,
uplift you.

Respect you boundaries

Don't let anyone get
comfortable disrespecting
YOU

Be mindful of your area & perimeter

Reflection

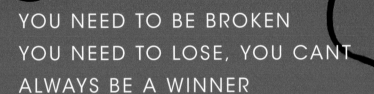

YOU NEED TO BE BROKEN
YOU NEED TO LOSE, YOU CANT
ALWAYS BE A WINNER

Channel your Emotions

WHEN YOU HAVE
VICTORY YOU
UNDERSTAND WHAT'S
IT LIKE TO WIN WITH
CLASS

Intuition

Win with Dignity

WIN & HELP SOMEONE ELSE WIN ON THE WAY

Focus on exactly what you last
and IMPROVE and GROW
Be for YOU, not against you.

Get you mind right this season

Practice clear thinking and be
with YOU are called to be

Intuition

Give yourself a crown

Give yourself credit for the days you've made it when you thought you couldn't. GOD is going to use your past experiences to propel you in the future.

GOD will never leave us nor forsake us. He is present, gracious and good.

THE EVENT IS AFTER YOUR UNDERSTANDING

Stop sleeping on yourself
and push yourself like never
before. Make room for
GOD to invade your fears.

STOP BEIGN AFRAID POTENTIAL

Understanding Heart

UNDERSTANDS MEANS TO HEAR

God is a HEALER, PROVIDER, WAY-MAKER

FOR EVERY HEART GIVE THEM WISDOM

GOD is a redeemer

Don't believe the lie of the enemy

The enemy's number one tactic is
to have you, not know who YOU are.
The enemy is scared of you having
PURPOSE.

OBEY GOD FLAT-FOOTED

WHEN YOU WALK INTO A ROOM MOUNTAINS START TOO MOVE

Break Generational Curses

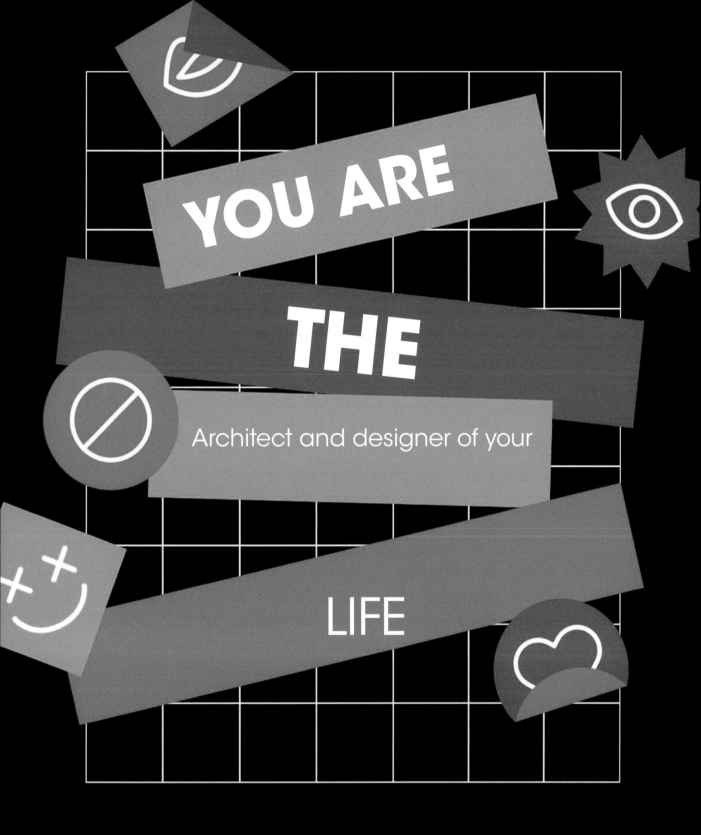

YOU ARE

THE

Architect and designer of your

LIFE

ROOKING STATUS

Do not be anxious about anything,
but in every situation, by prayer
and petition, with thanksgiving,
present your request to God.

- Philippians 4:6

If worry counted as a spiritual gift, I would be a spiritual
giant! I can't count the hours and energy wasted
on worrying about what might happen, what could
happened or even what could even happen… I am
through with worry! As of right now I'm turning over
a new leaf. I'm turning in my Master Worrier status in
exchange for a Rookie Truster status. I'll accept the
rookie status because I know it is going to be a journey
to learn to trust God in all aspects of life.

Trust the one who loves me more that I can imagine.
Trust the all-powerful, omnipotent God. Do you
want to join me in exchanging worry to trust?

SMILE OF LOVE

Love is patient, love is kind, it does
not envy, it does not boast, it is not
proud. It does not dishonor others,
it is not self seeking, it is not easily
angered, it keeps no record of wrongs.

-1 Corinthians 13:4

Show love to yourself. Show even
more love to others. Sprinkle kindness
to strangers. Humans are always
in need of love. Surround yourself
with love. BE LOVE. Be LIGHT. Be the
change in the world and show that
love, that so many are afraid of
revealing. Who was the bright genius
that said anyone who shows love is
"weak" did anyone check the sources
on that? Was that person hurting and
craving love they never received.

LOVE

REAL ABUNDANCE

Dear friends, let us love one
another, for love comes from God.
Everyone who loves has been
born of God and knows God.

- 1 John 4:7

The way of our world, especially in America, is to work hard and make lots of money in order to buy lots of things. We want more, more and more. There is even a sense of failure if we do not have the "things" that those around us have. But what is real abundance? Clear your mind for the moment of the gadgets, toys and things that are already in your possession or on your wish list. What is left in your life that really matters? This is the abundance you should concentrate on – a strong relationship with your God; opportunities to serve Him and others; family and friends who love you. Abundance is not really "stuff" it is relationships beginning with God and then moving on down the list. Don't let your focus get stuck an accumulating things that keep you equal with others in the world's eyes. Focus on relationships that's true abundance.

ABUNDANCE

NEW PATHWAYS

If anyone, then knows the good
they ought to do and doesn't
do it, it is sin for them.

- James 4:1

Life is not static, it is always changing so if you aren't
willing to change with it, you will be left doing the
same old same old. Learn a new skill. Master a new
computer program. Take dance lessons. Volunteer for
the refugee ministry at your church. Try something new.
Yes, it will be a process to learn it, but as you learn from
day to day, you will grow and change.

FRESH AIR.

SPREAD KINDNESS

If you can maintain a positive attitude and make a real effort to treat all you meet with love and kindness, that will also spread to others. What a joy to be able to spread the love of God to all you meet. By allowing God's love to flow through you so that you are a blessing to others so the will be better off by being around you and absorbing your presence.

WORK IN PROGRESS

Right now is all we have. How are you going to use it.

We only have the moment that exists right now. After you ask yourself how are you going to use it. Think about if what you decided is worth it when your time stops ticking. That beef you have carried for so long. Is it worth it? That person you wish you had more time with but you never picked up the phone to call or text. Was it worth it. Death doesn't have to knock on your door if it's already been beside us our whole lives. With everything that's going to do with the moment you have? Rest in love to those who are no longer here and Live in peace to those who are. This is your moment. Make it count.

ACCEPTANCE

Finding the pleasure in pain

Pain is inevitable… not everyday
will be great day & even if my bad
days outweigh my good days,
no need to fall apart for I'll be
blessed twice for the mishap.

Pain is a feeling that many try to avoid but what if
we tried to hug pain, welcome pain with open arms
understanding that this is NOT the end. We are so used
to turning our backs on pain and not accepting the
change when pain itself is a blessing in disguise. Turn
that pain into purpose. Turn that pain into passion.

INEVITABLE

CONQUER

Be for yourself never against yourself.

Hey I get it. You have a fear. You area afraid to take the step or do things you don't know how to. Well let me tell you this, instead of being afraid of the fear, how about making the fear afraid of your. Now go conquer that obstacle and be great.

Printed in the United States
by Baker & Taylor Publisher Services